THE POWER OF "INNER SELF"

Manual for Operating from within your Inner Self

Aditya Chandrashekar

Chennai • Bangalore

CLEVER FOX PUBLISHING
Chennai, India

Published by CLEVER FOX PUBLISHING 2023
Copyright © Aditya Chandrashekar 2023

All Rights Reserved.

Paperback ISBN: 978-93-56483-06-4
Hardback ISBN: 978-93-56484-32-0

This book has been published with all reasonable efforts taken to make the material error-free after the consent of the author. No part of this book shall be used, reproduced in any manner whatsoever without written permission from the author, except in the case of brief quotations embodied in critical articles and reviews.

The Author of this book is solely responsible and liable for its content including but not limited to the views, representations, descriptions, statements, information, opinions and references ["Content"]. The Content of this book shall not constitute or be construed or deemed to reflect the opinion or expression of the Publisher or Editor. Neither the Publisher nor Editor endorse or approve the Content of this book or guarantee the reliability, accuracy or completeness of the Content published herein and do not make any representations or warranties of any kind, express or implied, including but not limited to the implied warranties of merchantability, fitness for a particular purpose. The Publisher and Editor shall not be liable whatsoever for any errors, omissions, whether such errors or omissions result from negligence, accident, or any other cause or claims for loss or damages of any kind, including without limitation, indirect or consequential loss or damage arising out of use, inability to use, or about the reliability, accuracy or sufficiency of the information contained in this book.

For direct inquires with Inner Self Movement you may Watsapp: +971507020914

Inner Self practical techniques helps you realize your highest potential by enabling you to operate through your "Inner-Self".

TABLE OF CONTENTS

Introduction 1
Nature of Self 5
Who Am I? 9
The Root of Happiness 10
Ways to Increase Prana 15
Beyond Thought Waves of the Mind 19
The Illusion of Time 25
Cultivate Habits to Operate from Your Inner Self 29
We are all ONE 33

INTRODUCTION

I was born in this current physical body in the south Indian state of Tamil Nadu in a town called Rajapalayam, into a family rooted in tradition. Growing up my childhood days were influenced by my parents, grandmother and my brother.

The days with my grandmother were filled with her teaching me mantras, music, Surya namaskar and pranayama. My grandmother and my brother played a big part in shaping my core values and my awareness of the Self. She named me Chandrashekar after her Guru, fondly known as the Kanchi Maha periyava (The Great being from Kanchi) by the people of Tamil Nadu. Every time I touched her feet to take her blessing as is customary in any home in India, she would apply tilak on my forehead and tell me, "Chandra, you need to uphold the honor of the family and the values."

As a playful child, I never took her seriously during my school days. I was among the most mischievous children in my class. I was not that keen on studying the curriculum books so I wouldn't do well in the exams. Teachers liked to keep me out of the class so peace could prevail inside the class. I was good at sports because it felt lively. I could channel all my energies in one thing, when i run there was no thinking, the body moved automatically" there was no awareness of time, i would realize that i won the race only after the race was over. Sports kept me in the present and allowed me to test the limits of mind and body. I loved 100-meter races and athletics in general.

Meanwhile my brother was suffering from a rare type of illness which no doctor could Identify, he couldn't walk or talk or communicate, but he looked totally fine. With radiant eyes and bright, sharp features he seems to be exactly like Gautama the Buddha. He was bedridden and my beloved parents had looked after all his needs meticulously throughout his life. An astrologer predicted at the time of my brother's birth, that he was a yogi in the past life and due to an untimely death in his past life he had to re-incarnate once again just to finish the remainder of his past life. And he had chosen a birth without any positive or negative karma. Hence, he was born in this state, and the astrologer told my parents to come back after 13 years. He didn't predict anything else. I was called by my principal in the middle of a math class to go home immediately. To my shock, i found my brother had passed away. I realized my mom was doing her pooja at the time of his death and a meditator by the name of Radha came home and rang the bell to inform my mom that my brother had passed away. Radha had an instinct during meditation that he had passed away and alerted my mom. Just as the astrologer had predicted my brother passed away in his 13th year

With all this happening around me, I had a few important questions unanswered. The need to know the answers to these questions were burning inside me by the time i finished my schooling:

How was an astrologer able to predict the death of my brother accurately?

How did a person who was not in the same home knew my brother had passed away ?

Where was I before I was born?

What determined my current birth ?

What happens to me after I die?

What is the purpose of this life?

Who am I?

Introduction

After my schooling in Rajapalayam, I had to travel to Chennai to do my under graduation. Suddenly, I had to stay in a college hostel and had plenty of time to find the answers to these questions. As I did my daily college duties, I slowly started to buy books related to spirituality and visited many places in and around Chennai to find answers. I was one of the few students in my class who got placed in the campus recruitment. After a couple of years, I moved to Abu Dhabi for my work.

Once I came to Abu Dhabi, I had a deep spiritual quest. I had one month off every year to go to India. Every year I went, I would find guru by coincidence and ask them several questions. One led to another and the more I searched the more questions I had unanswered.

This went on every year from 2012. This search was mainly to find out Who am i ? If I find someone who can teach me, ill approach and learn from them. I attended a 10-day silent Vipassana practice with my family and it was an eye opener and nourished my soul and gave me enough motivation to learn more. Over the course of the next 10 years i would learn various techniques of meditations from my gurus and would practice it with the same dedication i would practice for my 100-meter races

On one of my trips back from Shiridi to Abu Dhabi, I didn't have prasad to share with my friend so I closed my eyes and sent prayer to Shiridi Sai baba to give me some prasad. As soon as this prayer, when I had a conversation to a random person sitting next to me in the Pune airport He introduced himself as Prasad. I felt baba has answered my prayers and given me a person by name Prasad. I had an instinct this is something special.

Prasad asked me, "What is your life purpose? What are your interests?"

I told him, "My purpose is to know who I am, what is your purpose?"

He said, "My purpose is to serve people in every way possible through action."

Service through action was his policy and he still lives by this policy.

When he knew my life purpose, Prasad invited me to teach his people in Bangalore how to meditate and initiate them into some spiritual practices. He offered to cover the expenses for my trip from Abu Dhabi to Bangalore and asked only one thing in return, "Can you teach my people how to meditate?"

I eagerly accepted and was excited about this opportunity. We fixed the dates. Prasad arranged all the logistics and coordination with the participants for a well-planned 3-day silent retreat we both travelled to Bangalore just to conduct silent mediation for 3 days. I was able to connect with the higher self and there was a free flow of understanding of Truth and firsthand experience of inner self. The participants cried with tears of joy by the end of this 3 days and elders who were aged 70+ said they never felt such joy in their life and were full of gratitude for organizing this meditation. At the final day when we did a Nature meditation to thank nature, nature blessed us back in no time and it rained immediately while we were meditating. Water drops seeped through the hut and fell on all of us. I had a profound sense of unity with nature, the energy was all encompassing my body got multiple goosebumps and was overwhelmed by the experience.

The search for the Truth has culminated in me wanting to share what I found in this book. ***The Power of Inner Self*** gives direction to a seeker who is in search of absolute truth. This book is not meant to be read like a story This book should be felt with the soul, experienced with the heart and the exercises given must be made your everyday habits for you to get the most out of this Inner- Self manual.

My humble gratitude to all beings that ever lived, to all beings that are living and to all beings that will ever live for guiding me through this journey. I thank the all encompassing energy field which holds all of animate and inanimate energy together, i thank this energy which made all of creation possible

NATURE OF SELF

The true purpose of life is the realization of the self.

The "Self" transcends the thought waves in the mind. The "Self" transcends the limitations of the body.

When the body is still without any movement and when there are no thought waves in the mind, the True Self which is ever present within us can be experienced.

A person who has transcended the thought waves of the mind and abides in his consciousness can experience heightened awareness of himself.

Abiding in our consciousness is to be free from all polarities.

Bhagavan Shri Ramana Maharishi advised those who visited him to enquire about the True Self by a simple question, **"Who am I?"** until we find the answer.

Ask your thoughts, to whom have you arisen?

– Ramana Maharishi.

Exercise To identify Self:

Step 1.

Non-identification of self with the ever-changing aspects of our existence. Anything which changes is not your Self.

Example: Mind and its perceptions, bodily sensations both pain and pleasure, thought waves, emotions, attachments and aversions, past memory and future expectations, verbal delusion, right knowledge and wrong knowledge, time and information acquired through the 5 senses.

Step 2:

After a successful non-identification, what shines from within is the experience of your True Inner Self.

This Inner Self can be experienced if you identify with the awareness which is always present within you in the background in all three states of existence (wake state, dream state and sleep state).

Once the self is experienced it brings a sense of wholeness which is all-encompassing like the ether. Self is everywhere but can't be pinpointed in one place.

Self cannot be accurately described, but only be experienced. When you watch within yourself, Observe the awareness that is watching your thoughts, at this moment you are established within your Inner Self.

The Pretend Self (I) and Its Identification:

When we say "I am" followed by any statement it's called the pretend self.

The True Self is beyond the I and My, we and ours, they, and theirs.

The pretend 'I' arises out of ego and associates itself with ever-changing thought waves.

One should actively discard and eliminate this "pretend I".

It's easy to identify this "pretend I". See what this "I" clings to before it manifests.

This "I" can't exist on its own, it always needs to cling itself to something else for it to manifest.

What can be monitored can be improved upon, by monitoring our thoughts as it arises, we can observe it and identify the root cause of these thoughts.

The Self is just a witness to these thought waves, but never a participant to the thought waves. The Self cannot be identified with thoughts. It is beyond thoughts and associations. The Self is the one that there is. Self is always in a constant state of bliss.

The Self is an awareness in an awakened state continuously and consistently.

Yet the self is not the "I" which we often associate with, like I am strong, I am fit and healthy, I am happy and blissful, I am wealthy and generous.

If you pay attention and look closely, the "I" in these statements cannot manifest independently. "I" is dependent upon what they cling to, in this case, they are clinging to strong, fit, healthy, happy, blissful, wealthy and generous.

This pretend "I" cannot be mistaken as self.

These identities are mind-evaluated utility identities. This 'I' exists until it serves the utility for which it manifested for.

When the "I" cling to anything which is changing it is false.

By reasoning, if "I" is followed with an unchanging constant, we establish the "I" with the real self.

Example: I am consciousness; I am Self.

Therefore, the true "I" is the awareness of the Self.

When the self is experiencing itself, its just present in the moment.

This self is always present, irrespective of what happens in the outside world.

It is present in the background, irrespective of the thought waves in the mind.

It is present in the background when you are in deep sleep.

It is present even after you die.

It is present even before your birth.

Birth and death are only for the Body and mind. Not the self.

The self has no beginning and no end.

The Self is the only constant and hence your only intelligent choice is to identify yourself with your Inner Self.

Self is both all encompassing and nothing.

WHO AM I?

*P*onder this question long enough sincerely to know the answer all by yourself. There are no shortcuts to find this.

When you find it by yourself it leaves you with freedom.

But when someone tells you who you are it's just another theory until it is felt experientially.

However, let's see a few pointers in the right direction for you to do the finding experientially.

Exercise:

Step 1: When you attempt to answer the question who am I, you start by saying I am (....) And follow up with an answer.

Step 2: See if what is followed with, I am (...) is changing or unchanging.

Step 3: If it's changing then it's not true

Step 4: If it's unchanging then it's true.

THE ROOT OF HAPPINESS

Whenever we are happy, our acceptance level of what has happened in that moment of time is 100% and because we have completely accepted what has happened, we are happy. We were looking forward to what has happened and when it happens, we are happy because we have programmed our mind to accept only the desired result and when the desired result occurs, we are naturally happy.

When our awareness is focused on the positive aspects of the any situation, our mind instantly generates the benefits of the situation and tends to be happy until the awareness is focused on what has been perceived to have happened as positive and beneficial. Only a positive outcome becomes reality and happiness remains.

When our awareness is focused on the negative aspects of any situation, our mind instantly generates all things which can go wrong due to what has happened until the awareness is focused on what has been perceived to have happened as negative. Then fear, panic and misery follow.

Follow the middle path, where you recognize that everything that has happen is teaching you a lesson for your soul development. Look at the bigger picture, instead of zooming into the problem, zoom out and train your awareness to see the lessons learnt. Send gratitude and be in the middle path.

In the middle path, you won't be too happy after a success as you recognize that it's just a part of the journey. You won't be sad after a failure as you recognize that it has thought you more lessons than victories.

Just by widening your understanding by going deeper into the subject you can no longer take sides if its write or wrong , good or bad , yes or no and you will move beyond these polarities and you will be left only with a divine understanding of everything that there is. When you see the bigger picture, and remove the veils of limited perceptions of your eyes, you are now into the realm of divine understanding, this leads you directly into the middle path

Acceptance of the present moment is the root of Happiness.

You accept not because you are happy to accept, or because you like what the result is. You accept because you have no other choice. As the event has already occurred, you fully become aware that you cannot go back in time and change what has already happened in the past and change the result. Hence you accept it with an understanding that it can be improved upon in your next attempt.

Cultivating a habit of acceptance of what has happened in the past and in the present, without identifying with the result or outcome enables us to respond with the right action and experience constant peace and happiness within.

Happiness is not an acquired state of being, it is our natural state of being if we don't clutter your natural state of awareness with thoughts and corresponding emotions only happiness remain.

A simple example: Initially, it was very difficult for me to get a parking spot in the city, and I used to logically calculate that I may not get a parking spot in a crowded area and I had to wait for 10 minutes to 15 minutes to get a parking spot. Once I made up my mind to believe from now on wherever I go, I always get a parking spot whenever I want wherever I go, guess what, once I truly believed in this, it came into reality.

Ever since I decided to shift my thought process and believed that I get space to park wherever I go, I now get a parking spot every single time I want to park.

Acceptance only occurs when there is an understanding that what has happened taught me the lesson I need to learn and therefore you can only be filled with gratitude for the valuable lesson and hence accept it wholeheartedly.

Acceptance also happens when we have given gratitude for the situation which has already happened. Gratitude comes with acceptance.

All past experiences dose one of the following:
1) They have given you an experience.
2) They have taught you a lesson.
3) They have given you an understanding as per the awareness you had at that point in time.

The dominant belief of undercurrent Happiness:

When we get down to the bare Truth, it's easy to find when we wake up in the morning, after a deep sleep we feel energetic, fresh, and relaxed, this is because we just woke up in our original state of being. Once we wake up our mind starts bringing out our dominant beliefs, and habitual thought patterns. This literally distorts and covers the Self like a smoke screen, just like thick dust covers a diamond.

Our duty is to uncover the dust, so the true splendor and awe of the diamond naturally emerges. You are not making any efforts to polish the diamond, just by getting rid of the dust the natural splendor is revealed.

The Self is always present. Self is the awareness you had when you were born, Self is the awareness you will have even after death, it is the same awareness you had in all your past births.

Exercise: Before you open your eyes every morning, recognize you are the Supreme Divinity within and identify yourself with the ever present awareness within.

When you wake up recite the below affirmations:

I am that Self which is beyond mind and body.

I am that Self which has no beginning and no end.

I am the super-conscious bliss which is complete unto itself.

Cultivate awareness of Self to experience bliss.

What are Truth and Un-truth?

Observe the thought occurring in the present moment.

Identify if this thought is true.

Truth is Always constant.

Untruth is Ever changing.

Observe if the thought is always constant over a period and if the thought is unchanging, it can be identified to be true. If your thought satisfies the above criteria, your thought is identified with the Truth.

If the thought is identified with anything which keeps changing, then it is not true. Hence, we need to label this thought as untrue. Such thoughts lead to Misery.

Exercise:

Witness the thought waves and find out if the present thought wave is rooted in Truth or Untruth.

Once you find the difference between the true and the untrue, it's easy to drop the Untruth and focus on the truth.

The trick is to drop the Truth as well. Now both Truth and Untruth are dropped.

Both truth and untruth is a result of limited perception of the reality" We have assigned to what has happen in a raw state to be true or untrue, If we can witness what has happen even without assigning truth and untruth or good and bad, we have the possibly to operate beyond the realm of the mental traps of the mind .

You are just there in the present without waiting for the 5 senses to bring more information. Now you have no thought to catch, as you have dropped all mental activity you are being made aware of the breath in this present moment. As you look within, even the breath is forgotten.

What remains is the awareness of the Self. You are just there doing nothing, dropping all thoughts and just being in the present.

WAYS TO INCREASE PRANA

Prana is the energy body without which our physical body can't exist. Prana Sakthi simply means life force energy in our body. Prana means Life force. Without Prana one is considered dead. Sakthi means Power. Prana Sakthi is life force energy required for the optimal functioning of our Mind, body and Spirit complex. Kids have high Prana Sakthi, this keeps them energetic, enthusiastic, and lively. Optimal amount of Prana in our body is the key for life to happen in the present moment.

High Prana Sakthi in our body directly aids us in spiritual progress. Therefore, spiritual practice is meant to be done when you are having high prana in your body when your mind and body are at its peak. It's easier to focus on a single thing, inward or outward if your physical and mental health is good.

An increase of Prana:

- Aids the immune system and keeps the body healthy.
- Keeps the mind fresh and helps to walk in the middle path.
- Allows you to be in an energetic state. And live a long life.

How to Obtain Prana Sakthi from the 5 Elements:

Element	Intake	Details	Best practice
Earth	Raw food	Fruits, vegetables, nuts and greens, and a plant-based diet is preferred.	Eat only when you are hungry. Eat raw food and ask yourself if the food has Prana in it. Plant-based diet.

Water	Water	Untreated natural stream water or water energized with positive words written next to them for at least 24 hours before drinking.	Write prayers and allow the water to read positive words and intentions overnight before you drink.
Fire	Physical work	Surya Namaskar, Yogic exercises, outdoor physical games.	Physical activity in nature. Working with nature. Connecting with the SUN by direct sun gazing, just after sunrise and just before sunset. Watch the tip of a burning flame of an oil lamp
Air	Breathing	Pranayama	Working towards your life purpose and Yogic breathing (When you breathe in watch your lungs and belly expand outwards like a balloon, when you breathe out, let your lungs and belly contract inwards).
Ether	Deep sleep	Natural deep sleep, doing nothing. Paying attention to the sky and the cosmos.	Sleep, meditation & Samadhi.

The key to Prana is to do what you love, naturally we are enthusiastic and enjoy what we do, we breathe well and have a relaxed mind. This automatically keeps the Prana at an optimal level.

Awareness in the present moment will increase Prana. When we are in a relaxed state, we are comfortable and naturally, the Prana Sakthi does not deplete, it is maintained at an optimal level.

Formula:

Smile and accept the present moment immediately with all your heart. This leads to a relaxed mind and body.

Find Your Vision & Purpose:

A vision is the aim of a higher purpose which benefits the Self which in turn is beneficial to humanity either with the well-being of their mind, body and Spirit or the upliftment of their capabilities.

When you have a purpose in life, a vision to strive towards this automatically aligns all your actions towards fulling your vision, you are aware that it will lead towards your goal, hence you will find the strength and motivation required to perform these actions. The journey is fully alive and filled with excitement. Irrespective of the end result the entire journey towards the goal becomes a celebration. Your entire mind , body and spirit will be filled with prana if you enjoy the journey of your life

A good vision impacts all beings in a positive manner. Solves a problem which directly enhances the well-being of existence the mind, body, and Spirit. The journey towards the Purpose must serve all the 5 koshas in a human being.

1) Annamaya kosha – Gross physical body intake of the right kind of nourishing food.
2) Pranamaya Kosha – Energy body through increasing the Prana Shakthi in the body through breathing like a baby.
3) Manaonmaya kosha – Feeding the mind with thoughts which are in alignment with the purpose of the soul and just being a witness to the rest of the thought waves.
4) Vignanamaya kosha – Using intellect to discern what is required and executing free will based on right knowledge to develop beneficial habits.
5) Aananthamaya kosha – Bliss arising when you are one with your Inner Self.

Realizing one's true Inner Self is one of the greatest visions or goals that there is.

It brings peace, happiness, and harmony within oneself. These same qualities will naturally manifest on the outside as well. You are fulfilled unto yourself.

Once we are aligned with the Inner Self, we automatically operate in alignment with our soul's purpose of incarnating on Planet Earth. This also benefits everyone around us.

When you are nothing, you become everything; When you are everything you become nothing;

Watch the air flow in your breath, feel it expand the belly and the lungs and feel the air revitalize your entire being in every breath. Just by being aware of the air flow in your present breath Prana is regularized automatically

BEYOND THOUGHT WAVES OF THE MIND

Going beyond the thought waves of the mind leads to the space where the Self is experienced. Yoga is nothing but being one with the true Self. Yogic practices are intended to experience the real Self.

Every thought wave we have creates a ripple effect throughout the universe. First, it impacts our body and then it impacts our immediate surroundings. Gradually, it travels full circle through the cosmos.

Patanjali Maharishi has thought us there are five kinds of thought waves:

1) Right knowledge – When what is thought corresponds to reality.
2) Wrong knowledge – When what is thought does not correspond to reality.
3) Verbal delusion – Confusion arising due to incorrect representation of Truth.
4) Sleep – Is a single continuous thought about nothingness.
5) Memory – Is when past perceptions come back to present awareness.

Thoughts have tremendous power, beyond what we can imagine. Thought is the basis of all creative and destructive power.

All that which is existing now was once a thought wave which went on to be manifested into a reality.

Just by paying attention to our thoughts in the present moment with full awareness and asking a few simple questions, we can filter all unwanted thought waves.

Exercise:

Is this thought seeing things in its true form as it is?

Is this thought beneficial to me ?

Is this thought helpful to reach my goal of realizing myself?

Is this thought because of my past habit pattern or is it because I wanted it with my free will?

With persistent observing of thoughts, you will soon notice that gradually you will be left with only thoughts which are beneficial to you, and the thoughts which will be helpful in achieving your goals.

But when the goal is beyond the material plane and if the goal is to realize our true self, even the beneficial thoughts must be neutralized. All thoughts must come to a halt. The thought of self-introspection, the thought of observing the observer must also stop and the moment this is achieved, automatically what is left over is the radiance of the Self.

What happens next , ill leave it for you to experience

By cultivating awareness and training the awareness to witness the thoughts consciously though this alone is not sufficient. This will drastically reduce the amount of unwanted thought patterns and sail the mental ship in the direction we want it to go, rather than being driven in the direction of the storm of the unchecked mind.

To witness your true self, you must not identify with the thought waves occurring through the 5 sense perceptions and attain total freedom from neither desire nor aversion with thought waves arising from the 5 senses, past memory, future imagination, ignorance and identification with Untruth or false I.

Karma is nothing but repetitive persistent thought waves which triggers an emotional charge. These thoughts are like a stone thrown in the pond, emotional charges of the thought is similar to the ripples created by the stone. You cant expect the ripples to stop by picking the same stone once again from pond.

At the time of death, if there are unresolved or unsatisfied thought waves which are still persistent, these thought waves are retained and finds a way to fulfill them in its next incarnation. The Karmic thought waves keep you in the cycle of birth and death continuously until this cycle is broken by neutralizing all thoughts.

So just by learning about the nature of mind which is nothing but just thoughts and perceptions, nothing more and by practicing being the witness to it, you can release yourself from the cycle of birth and death

If one's goal is not to be born again and be fully realized, then the first thing one needs to do is to resolve all their persistent thoughts through acceptance and not identifying with this thought. Any thought which comes with a lot of baggage must be immediately identified with karma and action must be taken to resolve it and come to a neutral state with this thought, so it doesn't come back to your awareness.

Exercise to transcend beyond mind : Watch the thoughts as they occur do not assign any significance to the thought. Just watch it as it is. Witness the thought in its raw form. Realize that just by mere witnessing you are no longer the participant in the thought. At this point you become the witness. Hence any thought which has arisen is just a passing cloud in the back ground sky of the witness

Watch your breath:

Breath and mind are intertwined like two threads of the same rope. The mind has tied layers of this rope around the Self, fully obstructing the view of the Self.

For us to simply untie them, we must keep vigil over the breath and its movement inside the body. This will untie the knots and peel the rope from obstructing the Self.

Exercise: Observe your breath and feel the airflow entering the nostril, follow its path through the lungs, feel the stomach come out when inhaled, feel the air turn around and observe the airflow exiting the nostril.

When the breath is observed, naturally the breath becomes deeper and slower. This automatically calms down the mind.

Once the incoming breath and the outgoing breath are neutralized, you are totally free of mind. All you are left with is void of just being, without any contamination of sense perceptions, and without any plays of thought waves in the mind.

How does one neutralize the incoming and the outgoing breath?

Step 1: Observe the airflow in your nostrils as it goes in and as it comes out.

Step 2: Witness the gap between the inhaled breath and the exhaled breath.

Once you have felt this gap between the breath, automatically your awareness will be in this gap; The awareness of the air flow in the breath and the sensation of inhaling and exhaling will stop completely.

Your awareness can't be simultaneously both at the breath and the gap. Once the gap is witnessed it stays. Again, you feel the breath and the mind starts functioning. This is totally fine, accept this as a natural state and continue to witness the gap between the breaths.

Witness your breath as you wake up in the morning, witness it when you take a bath, when you brush your teeth, when you walk, when you dress up, when you eat, when you sit, when you lie down, when you sleep, when you move, when you are doing something or when you are in between a busy day. Witness the space whenever you can throughout the day. This will make you more aware of your thoughts and your surroundings. This will bring your awareness to the present moment.

Watching the breath will bring a state of peace to your daily activities. It will relax you immediately and automatically all thoughts disappear. The flow of Prana is increasing every time you witness your breath. High Prana keeps the thoughts and feelings in a state of high vibration, beneficial to us. Prolong it and thoughts stop. You are just there, without thought. Thinking has stopped automatically. You don't force anything. It happens naturally.

A life lived with awareness is like being re-born and taking a re-birth, it is erasing all the past and being totally in the present moment. It's starting on a clean slate. Every time we are aware of the Self, we rub the slate clean and start fresh.

A life happening like this is a state of a yogi. The great Patanjali puts it "Yoga is control of thought waves in the mind". To establish mastery over the mind, body and Spirit, you must start watching the breath.

Slow down to anchor with your Inner Self:

Know that slowing down is a gift:

To slow down the thought waves of the mind, you must zoom out of the thought and not be identified with the thought. Just watch the thought as a witness. The Self is the witness of everything, it's the background awareness of all three states—awake state, dream state and deep sleep state.

Just as the ship is anchored to a solid base, and is not affected by the passing storm, when the awareness is anchored with the witness, the storm of thought waves can't affect us in any way. As thoughts come in, it passes away. It has no effect on us because we choose to identify with the Self and not the thought.

Step 1: Inhale slowly while moving both your hands upward as slowly as possible and exhale slowly bring both your hands downwards at an even slower pace and rest them on your lap.

Step 2: Watch the awareness within and just be yourself and do nothing.

Is Mind Real ? When you are a witness there is no mind. Mind dose not exist. Yet when you are thinking thoughts it seems to be real. When you are the self you cannot be mind. When you are the mind you cannot be self.

THE ILLUSION OF TIME

The present moment is where the creation happens, it's magical. The present is where the action happens. It's alive, and the present is the only time we have complete control over. Present is GOD's gift for us to be used wisely with our free will.

Every situation, all of history, all accomplishments, and all actions, has happened in the present moment of that time. It was done by someone else in their present, it may seem past now but as it happened it was happening in the present.

Anything which you have ever done, you were able to do it only in your present.

Our mind is tricking us to believe that it was our past. And anything from the past has no use in the present moment because it cannot be changed. But the past can always be improved upon, with the understanding that I can create a new chapter starting from the present moment.

The nature of time is infinite, it has no beginning, and it has no end. Time is an idea to measure periodic events and the attempt to manage time is futile. The more you attempt to manage time the more misery you create for yourself. Time cannot be managed; time can be used wisely in alignment with your goal by acting in the present moment.

Past and future are two imposters who take away our present. It takes away from what can be done in the present. Contemplating the past or imagining the future is taking away the magical moments present in the "Now" from us. Dwelling in the past cannot change anything in the past. Imagining our future goals is just fiction until it's acted upon in the present. Taking concrete action in the present moment will surely take us to the goals we set ourselves to achieve.

You can't manage time; you can only act in the present moment. Postponing is the trick of the mind to avoid the present moment. The mind likes to keep us in the comfort zone of inaction and past habit patterns, The minds re-creation of what is known is nothing but a repetition of the past.

The present moment in the NOW is all that there is. There is no such thing called "I have no time". We have all the time in the world. Instead of saying "I have no time" you must say i have infinite amount of time, what you have prioritized is exactly what you will be doing in the present. If you are wasting your time, then you have your past habits prioritized to waste time. It is the mind's convenient way to trick us and put the blame on time, instead of taking complete ownership of the results we are manifesting.

Anything we do with absolute involvement we do it with no reference to time. When i ran the 100- meter race there was no effort i was in the zone, Movement happen naturally. There was no thought. High-performing athletes, musicians, actors, artists, and dancers, ask anyone they would tell you they were in their natural zone, where time ceases to exist. When there is no awareness of time, they perform their best. This is when they have created history, and broken world records, their potential best has manifested when they had no sense of time whatsoever.

If you feel time is not moving quick enough and keep watching the time, this means you are not doing what you love. You must stop and ask yourself if what you are doing is really what you wanted to do or was it imposed on you by your surroundings.

Every human being is fully capable of experiencing this state of being in the present continuous or being zoned out while performing an action. This is a state we need to experience every minute, every hour, and every day throughout our life. This is the best way to manage time.

We have lived these moments in the present with complete involvement. Life has flourished and blossomed into a beautiful flower in these moments of greatness.

We all have experienced such times at least briefly in our lives when we felt no time. We say, "Oh time has passed so quickly that I didn't realize it passed by." When you meditate there is no time felt.

Whether you like it or not, whether you pay attention or not, time keeps giving us infinite moments of the present. So, there is no lack of time. Time is abundant beyond what you can ever use.

When you postpone something, know the very act of postponing is your habit pattern. And it creates a bad time for you.

Aligning our actions to our life purpose and the thing that every cell of us wants to achieve with emotion and thus creating laser-sharp focus is the best way to live in the present. Identify what you are good at and start doing it now, make it your life purpose.

This is a sure-shot way to live a life of no regrets as the actions which you want to take are being taken in the present moment and this cycle never stops.

A person who lives this way will be content and, on the move, living life to its full potential is the greatest good you do for your mind, body, and Spirit complex.

Repetition of these actions aligned to the Goal becomes our habit. Success is built on strong habits. Practice sessions the athletes go through are nothing but repetitive actions in the present moment toward their goal.

Through the clarity of Goal and persistent action we can stop procrastination and jump into constant action until the Goal is achieved. It is this fire of action which can burn all illusions of time. Keep this fire burning until your last breath. Make reaching your Inner Self your spiritual Goal. This is your birth right.

Time and self are identical. It can't be neither in the future nor in the past. It can only be felt and realized in the present.

Exercise: Act now

1) **Do what you really love to do from the bottom of your heart and experience the state of timelessness every day while you are doing it.**
2) **Love your self now, send love to all beings "Now". Be in bliss. "Now"**
3) **If you want to achieve your goal, start the action now. Because now is the best time to do it.**
4) **List down the top 10 things you always wanted to do but kept postponing it. Do it now. Action this list now, because now is the best time to do this.**

CULTIVATE HABITS TO OPERATE FROM YOUR INNER SELF

A habit is a repeated activity which happens in our day-to-day life in any of the following ways. Be mindful and aware of the following aspects which you repeat. Carefully cultivate beneficial habit patterns in each of the below to go deeper within.

1) Repetitive thoughts/intentions we think consciously or unconsciously (Identify with the Self).
2) Repetitive words we use consciously or unconsciously (Talk only Truth).
3) Repetitive actions we take consciously or unconsciously (Meditate and contemplate within).
4) Repetitive food we eat consciously or unconsciously (Eat pranic plant-based food).
5) Repetitive physical activities (Keep your body healthy).
6) Repetitive way of breathing consciously or unconsciously (Let your normal breath be yogic breath). Yogic breath is breathing like a baby, As you breath in your lungs and abdomen expands outwards, and as you breath out your stomach and lungs goes inwards

Focus all your awareness on what you want to do, intense focus on your goal will give you only the habits which are in sync with what you want to do. Automatically, all other habits which are not in alignment with your dominant goal will disappear.

Habits can be replaced with better habits, but they can never be fought and won over. Never try to fight a habit, just replace it with a desired habit.

Push and it comes close.

Anything you push away due to aversion or dislike will keep coming back to you just like a magnet.

Pull and it goes far.

Anything you pull towards you by force will not stay, you will find that it will go away the minute you stop pulling.

Find the middle path.

Finding the middle path happens naturally if you increase the number of different perspectives you come to understand and have a heightened awareness to see it in its entirety there cant be a judgment made out of the situation. On the other hand if you have made a verdict about the situation that means it has not taken into consideration all the aspects of the case in its entirety. Hence middle path is an outcome of heightened awareness of the situation.

Everything in nature is progressing in the middle path, not too quick and not too slow. Yet everything nature wants is accomplished in its own time. A new river is formed, A tree has grown and A forest has formed. We are a part of this nature and it's only natural for us to follow the middle path.

Be the witness:

Whatever happens on the outside, just be a witness to it. Don't be a participant and instead of identifying yourself with the situation happening outside, just watch it as a witness.

Watch the watcher within:

There is your awareness which is ever present while you're watching what you do throughout the three states of existence wake state, dream state and deep sleep state and deep sleep.

May the observer and the observed be one and the same. Direct your awareness on the awareness itself.

This habit will make you always become aware of your inner self, and you are more conscious and you will start noticing every thought wave which is arising within you. And just by noticing and not identifying with the thoughts gradually there are no thoughts and you become nothing.

Abandon all effort, Find the silence beyond thoughts then simply remain

Being in love with everything and everyone;

When you are no thought, you become love and the outcome is being in love with yourself, there is no division between you and the entire cosmos, your love for yourself is a love for the entire cosmos. You no longer see yourself as separate from anything.

This is not ordinary love, there is an universal aspect of this love which has the capacity to engulf everything in its path with love. This is devoid of any expectation or longing. This is pure love.

When you are one with your inner self , the outcome is you become embodiment of love.

Your understanding of everything has a deeper meaning and out of recognition of the true reality behind everything you start to love everything. You see all beings as a part of your own extension and love all beings.

Gratitude is the best prayer

Exercise:

Send gratitude in the following order:

1) **Gratitude to my mother, father and all my ancestors.**
2) **Gratitude to all human beings who ever lived, living and will ever live.**
3) **Gratitude to all living beings on Earth's plane.**
4) **Gratitude to everything, everyone, and all situations I experience in my past present and future.**
5) **Gratitude to my body, mind and Spirit.**
6) **Gratitude to the ever present awareness.**

May all beings be happy, peaceful and experience bliss.

Imagine these thought waves arising from the center of the heart and reaching all beings in consecutive waves of high energy frequencies.

May all beings be filled with love and light. Imagine a shower of love and light engulfing all beings throughout the cosmos.

Send gratitude to all living beings.

Treat everyone you meet with gratitude and find ways to help them in any way possible. Love all beings unconditionally

WE ARE ALL ONE

When the mind and body are transcended and when we no longer operate from the mind nor the body, we naturally are in a state of thoughtless nothingness. This is not nothing, this is everything.

In this state of experience, we are all connected, all beings are one, and every being is the extension of everyone else. This is the natural feeling which originates from within. Not only are we a part of everything, but we are also that thing we are describing. And similarly, everything is a part of us. "I" am a part of everything.

All divisions disappear naturally. We come to realize we are all one infinite energy. We are manifestations of love and light.

The awareness expands to the vastness of the Universe and everything that there is. Our mind loses its conditioning of being separated from everything and loses all separation and becomes all-encompassing.

Our temporary identities of I am a human, country, race, sect, religion, gender, beliefs, experience, accumulated tendencies, goals, and memory, all disappear, thereby eliminating all karma with cause and effect and the cycle of action and reaction is stopped. Differences disappear and Unity remains.

Future imaginations, everything vanishes when the awareness is directed toward the *Inner Self*. You become oneness. Rather you are experiencing the oneness for the very first time. It was always present waiting for you to realize it.

Just by touching this Oneness, all limitations are immediately abandoned by the mind and the self assumes its rightful state of Infinity

When you are nothing , you become everything ;

ABOUT THE AUTHOR

*E*xperiencing lasting peace and bliss within himself with the guidance of higher beings and gurus.

He enjoys being in the present And loves to share his experience and knowledge of how to just be yourself and to see everything as they are without any filters .

He has founded *"Inner Self Movement" to share the secret techniques to be in bliss forever.*

Through his direct satsangs and teachings he has guided and helped people overcome fear, anxiety, grief due to loss of a loved one, Physical illness and emotional pain and lead them towards clarity and wisdom. Enabled people overcome polarities and find their inner balance thereby establishing lasting peace within.

Most importantly Shree. Aditya has enabled people to find spiritual wellbeing by re-connecting with their Inner-Self.

'You are not born when your body is born, you are born when you find out who you really are, this is the day you realize you are ever present.'

'When you become nothing you are everything'

— Shree Aditya Chandrashekar

www.ingramcontent.com/pod-product-compliance
Lightning Source LLC
LaVergne TN
LVHW061623070526
838199LV00078B/7397